Fiona Tan
VOX POPULI
>>> *Sydney*

Book Works in association
with the Biennale of Sydney

PORTRAITS >>>

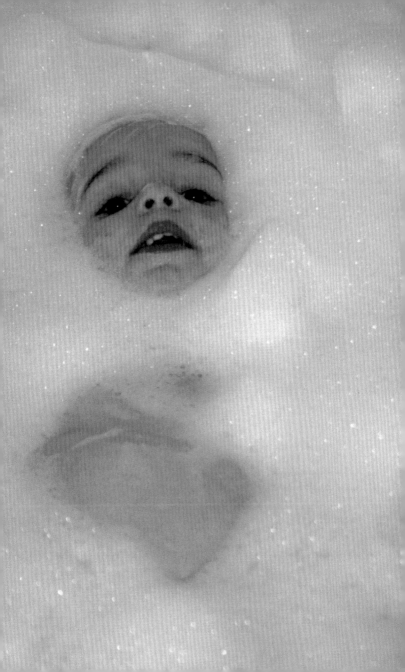

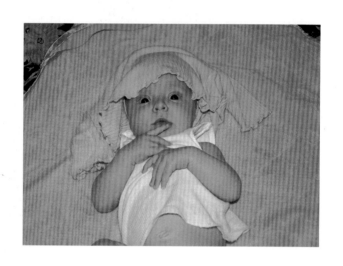

98

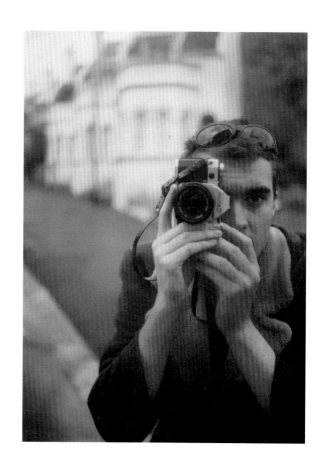

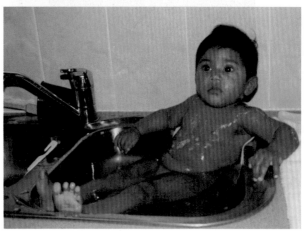

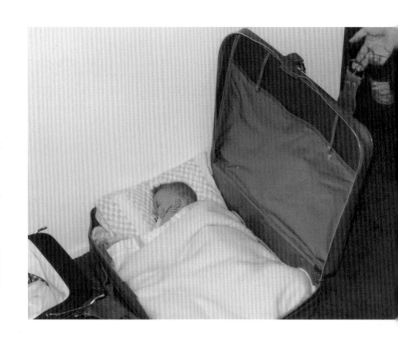

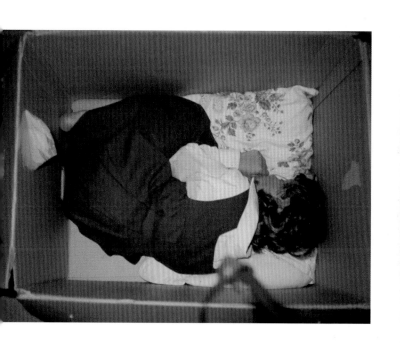

NATURE >>>

Mappo mundi
Fiona Tan's *VOX POPULI*

>>> Rachel Kent

Fiona Tan is an artist for whom the human subject is central. Working across the media of photography and film, she has created a diverse body of work that explores ideas about individual identity as well as its collective expression. Tan draws upon a range of references in the realization of her art: from archival or found film footage, to family photographic albums, to the still and moving imagery, she frequently records herself. Ranging from the anonymous and the historical to the highly personal and the contemporary, these works seamlessly interweave narratives in a play of private introspection and wider socio-political commentary.

Tan came to international prominence in the late 1990s with her incorporation of archival film footage depicting the nineteenth-century European colonial presence in Africa, Asia and the Pacific. Engaging with both documentary and anthropological traditions, her recuperation of anonymous footage in the single-screen projection *Facing Forward* [1999] drew attention to the camera's pivotal role in the colonial process with its objectifying and exoticising impulses. Preceding this work, Tan's one-hour documentary *May You Live in Interesting Times* [1997] sought to locate the artist's own identity in relation to her Chinese heritage, drawing upon family photographs spanning several generations. Based in Amsterdam and born in Indonesia to an Australian mother and ethnic-Chinese father, Tan is well positioned to comment on the complexities of culture and place as they shape individual identity. A further work in this series, *Thin Cities* [2000], presented found imagery from the Filmmuseum Archive, Amsterdam, across five suspended screens, documenting cultural communities and traditions around the world.

In her more recent work Tan has moved away from historical film footage and photography to focus on contemporary lives in communities immediately surrounding us. *Correction* [2004] is one of several recent projects that have seen the artist working with diverse communities, entering their lives with considerable empathy and subtlety – but without overt commentary. Lacking the didacticism of so many political gestures through art, it is instead understated in its reflection on individual 'invisibility' and organizational/corrective structures. A previous project, *Countenance* [2002], saw Tan document a wide cross-selection of individuals living in Berlin during her residency there, ordering them into categories and sub-categories according to social, cultural and professional niche. Like *Correction*, this work consisted of filmed portraits, presented like photographic imagery, in which people posed for a limited time before the artist's camera – their discomfort and self-awareness revealed by occasional twitches and fidgeting. Referencing August Sander and his extended visual compendium of portrait 'types' during Weimar Germany, *Menschen des 20. Jahrhunderts*, Tan's work sat between the evocation of individual identity and a mass-portrait of German citizens in the new millennium.

Tan returned once again to family photographic albums in her collective portrait *VOX POPULI, Norway* [2004]. Commissioned for the Norwegian Parliament House in Oslo, it comprised a collage of imagery volunteered by ordinary individuals across the country. This material was then edited by the artist into a communal statement chronicling the passage of life from birth through to adulthood, old age and death. Described by one writer as 'a "register of selfhood" with which we can all identify', offering something well beyond cold statistical data on population, economy or religious make-up,[1] it bridges individual and communal experiences while respecting the integrity of both.

1. Suzanne Cotter, 'Each and Everyone', *VOX POPULI, Norway*, Book Works, London 2006.

Created for the 2006 Biennale of Sydney, Tan's new installation and publication, *VOX POPULI, Sydney* [2006] follow similar principles in their assimilation of photo-album imagery treasured by diverse individuals who inhabit this city. Described by the artist as 'an interaction between the poetic and documentary', its enmeshing of private and public histories creates a compelling and revealing mass-portrait spanning the 1960s to the present day. Recalling Sander – or even Gerhard Richter with his vast 'Atlas' of places and themes – it offers a unique view of the world and the many people who inhabit it.

Tan's *VOX POPULI* projects mark the beginnings of a new working model for the artist, in which the photographic display and its textual documentation, a limited edition artist's book, form a dual artistic statement. Community and place are central in the works, despite the universality of their themes, and it is the idea of difference – as well as sameness or commonality – that links the Norwegian and Australian works so far. Further country or city-focused projects will extend the series, teasing out the themes of commonality and difference: and each forming a jigsaw piece in an ever-expanding *mappo mundi* by the artist. The term 'global village' is perhaps apt here, recalling the interconnectedness between places, as well as their unique characters and contours. From the cool light of Norway to the tropical heat of Sydney – or the geographic remoteness of the former to Tan's own identity to the specificity of the latter, as her mother's country of birth – ideas both general and specific are suggested.

Writing on Richter's *Atlas*, an encyclopedic assemblage of found, amateur, advertising and newspaper photographs, the critic Benjamin Buchloch noted: 'neither the private photo album of the amateur, nor the cumulative projects of documentary photography could identify the discursive order of this photographic collection'.[2] Supplanting the traditional atlas book with its focus on structured geographical and astrological data, Richter's *Atlas* archive is more a collective social document encompassing themes of banality and the everyday through to the events of history and nature of memory itself – a form of 'anomic' archive.[3] Unlike Richter's *Atlas*, Tan's *VOX POPULI* works loosen the rigidity of the grid as a means of display, presenting more informal groupings of photographs in serendipitous masses across the gallery wall. Accompanied by their individual books [Richter's *Atlas* also exists in book form] and sourced purely from private, amateur imagery, there is an unmediated intimacy to Tan's work that situates it between private moment and collective, public memory.

While the human subject forms a central thread throughout Tan's artistic

2. Benjamin H.D. Buchloch, 'Gerhard Richter's Atlas: the anomic archive' in Bruno Cora et al, *Gerhard Richter*, Centro per l'Arte Contemporanea Luigi Pecci, Prato, Italy, 1999, p.155.
3. Ibid., p.156.

practice, it is the notion of humanism itself that permeates these works. As with many [but not all] of Tan's film and photographic projects, the *VOX POPULI* works are silent, the images 'speaking' for themselves through individual placement, selective groupings, drifts and flows of imagery that form a language built upon perception and identification. Inviting associations and evoking memories on the part of the viewer, they are inherently fluid in meaning. In this regard a local viewer's interpretation will be shaped as much by recognition or the search for identifiable features, as a non-local's impartial observation or parallel yet different referents. Thus an image of a young Asian couple and baby posed before the low stone wall encircling Farm Cove, at the mouth of Sydney Harbour, might prompt a discussion of nearby landmarks including the Sydney Opera House and Botanic Gardens. It may equally speak of a new life within a faraway land. Other images speak conversely of universal or shared experience. In one such instance two unrelated photographs of family birthday celebrations, taken years apart, see their male subjects posed almost identically as they blow out the candles on their respective cakes. Scanning the flow of imagery, individual or family histories may also be mapped out from pregnancy and birth to childhood and maturity.

It is interesting to consider why Tan has chosen Norway and then the city of Sydney as her twin focuses, to date, for the *VOX POPULI* works.

Initiated through exhibition opportunities, the two projects and locations nonetheless bear comparison for the complexities they throw up in relation to centre and periphery, coloniser and colonized – and historically ingrained perceptions of Europe as the seat of culture, and Australia as a land of convicts. Human migratory patterns over the last century have profoundly shaped contemporary Australian identity as a home to diverse nationalities, while geographical positioning has seen a strong Asian influence reflected in population, trade and culture. This stands somewhat in contrast to the apparent visual homogeneity of the former work – featuring predominantly Anglo-Saxon subjects of northern European descent. As Suzanne Cotter observes, there is nothing 'obvious' to identify this location as Norway rather than, say, Germany, Britain or The Netherlands. Subtle indicators – visible perhaps only to those from the country itself – are however sporadically presented through costume and landscape, 'engag[ing] the viewer in a quasi-ethnography in which we are compelled to make certain judgements'.[4] Caucasian, Australian Aboriginal, Asian and Indian subjects all feature in the later work, representing just some of the diversity of contemporary Australian life.

Viewing *VOX POPULI, Norway* in the context of the subsequent Sydney installation, contrasts in topography are immediately apparent from mountainous landscapes and chilly snowfields to bright beach and ocean

4. Suzanne Cotter, 'Each and Everyone', *VOX POPULI, Norway*, Book Works, London 2006.

vistas. The sport and leisure activities that accompany these climates are well documented as are a range of universal social activities and family events that are interchangeable in terms of country or origin. Children playing in the bath, family car trips, fishing expeditions, domestic interiors, household pets including a much-loved python: all are documented with equal attention in both works. Viewing these intimate fragments, a kaleidoscope of emotion is evoked from nostalgia to empathy, identification and humour. Indeed, humour forms an undercurrent in a number of Tan's groupings, as subjects and themes flow serendipitously in and out of one another.

Tan's interest in the 'vox populi' expands her longstanding interest in the documentary tradition, in its most egalitarian form. Featuring the ordinary [wo]man – or voice on the street – chosen at random, or through selective process, it proposes a democratic social commentary that harks back to the artist's previous work with archival film footage; to *Correction* with its prison inmates and guards who volunteered their time and faces for her camera; and likewise *Countenance* before it, with its individually posed portraits and thematic groupings. Ordinary people, ordinary faces, individual lives and stories to tell – Tan's *VOX POPULI* works and wider practice suggest an endless capacity for social reflection through the prism of personal commentary.[5]

5. An edited version of this text appears in the Biennale of Sydney 2006 publication.

>>> THE ARTIST WISHES TO THANK:

KATE FORD

CHARLES MEREWETHER

KATRINA PYM

CHRIS FOX

BARBARA FLYNN

BIENNALE OF SYDNEY

FRITH STREET GALLERY, LONDON

RUBEN AND NIELS DIJKSTAL

SOEN HOUW AND LESLEY TAN

AND ALL THE CONTRIBUTORS TO *VOX POPULI, SYDNEY:*

HELEN BAILEY-COOKE, JONATHON BAILEY, ZANNY BEGG, LIAM BENSON, LESLEY BOURKE, JESSIE BRETT, LAUREN BROWN, BARBARA BRYAN, KATIE BRYANT, REBECCA BUSHBY, JANE BYRNE, LINDA CAGGIANO, JON CASHMAN, AMY CASHMAN, JOSEPHINE CLEMENTS, MATTHEW CONNELL, MARY CRANE, ANNETTE CRAWFORD, STEVE DAVIS, JOANNE DELZOPPO, EINAR DOCKER, SANDRA DONATO, CINDI DRENNAN, TRACY DUNCAN, ELEANOR ER, NALLY FEAR, ATHENA FIELD, BARBARA FLYNN, KATE FORD, ERIN GREATHEAD, ANGELA GRIMSDALE, MAY HANWELL, DOMINICA HERON, SAHAR HOSSEINABADI, YAWEN JANG, NATASJA JANG, HYACINTHA JANG, JOHN JOHNSON, PARIS KELLY, BENISON KILBY, LANI KILLHORN, ALICE KIM, CECILIE KNOWLES, PATRICIA KNOWLES, TARA KITA, EDDIE LAHM, JOY LAI, TIM LATHAM, MARGARET MAYHEW, SARINYA·MANAMUTI, STEPHANIE MAZURE, MALCOLM MCKERNAN, ZOH MCENALLY, DAMIAN MCDONALD, MARLYSSE MEDINA, NADIA MALJKOVIC, JOHN MIDDLETON, MARY MUNRO, PANDORA NGUYEN, IOULIA PANOUTSOPOLOUS, DILEP PANDAY, CINDY PIGOZNIS, SAHIL PRASAD, BRENDAN RALPH, RENATO RAMSAY, CHE RITZ, CARLY ROBERTSON, ALISON ROSS, MARIA RUGGERI, ELISE ROUTLEDGE, JAY RYVES, INGRID SANT, SIMON SCHWAB, TAMARA SIMS, JILDA SIMPSON, VICKY SKARLATOS, MATTHEW SHIELDS, LENA SMITH, IMMA THIEL, JOHN TOMC, DARKO VUKOBRAT, KARINA WADDELL, CLANCY WALKER, WENDY WALLS, MELANIE WATKINS, ROHAN WILSON, ANN YEALLAND

>>> At the invitation of the Biennale of Sydney Fiona Tan conceived
the art project *VOX POPULI, Sydney*. Tan has selected images from
private photo albums from approximately ninety inhabitants of Sydney
who generously agreed to participate in this project. The results are
a wall installation, *VOX POPULI, Sydney* [2006] and this publication.

Fiona Tan
VOX POPULI
>>> *Sydney*
Published and distributed by Book Works
19 Holywell Row, London EC2A 4JB
www.bookworks.org.uk

Picture editing by Gabriele Franziska Götz and Fiona Tan
Concept and design by Gabriele Franziska Götz
Printed by Rosbeek, Nuth NL

VOX POPULI, Sydney is the second book in a series that present
us with a 'snapshot' of a country or a community through
photographs from family albums collected by Fiona Tan.

Book Works is funded by Arts Council England.
This publication has been generously supported
by Rosbeek, Nuth [NL]; Austcorp Group Ltd., Sydney; and the Biennale of Sydney

ISBN 1 870699 94 7